Maths
made easy

Key Stage 2
ages 7-8
Beginner

Author and Consultant Sean McArdle

Certificate

Congratulations to ....
(write your name here)
for successfully finishing this book.

☆ *You're a star!* ☆

DK

Counting to 1000

Fill in the missing words and numbers in the boxes below.

250	300	350	
Two hundred and fifty	Three hundred	Three hundred and fifty	Four hundred
450	500	550	
	Five hundred	Five hundred and fifty	Six hundred
	700		800
Six hundred and fifty		Seven hundred and fifty	Eight hundred
850	900	950	1000
	Nine hundred	Nine hundred and fifty	

Which number has a value between 456 and 571? Circle the answer.

453   471   575   580   600   650

Comparing and ordering

Write these numbers in order of size, starting with the smallest.

| 431 | 678 | 273 | 586 | | 273 | 431 | 586 | 678 |

Write these numbers in order of size, starting with the smallest.

267	931	374	740				
734	218	625	389				
836	590	374	669				
572	197	469	533				
948	385	846	289				
406	560	460	650				
738	837	378	783				
582	285	528	852				
206	620	602	260				
634	436	364	463				
47	740	74	704				
501	150	51	105				
290	92	209	29				
803	380	83	38				
504	450	54	45				

Comparisons

Circle the numbers that are more than 207.

72

158

(210)

(230)

(208)

Circle the numbers that are more than 705.

834   698

711   590

812

Circle the numbers that are less than 512.

268   507

600   564

378

Circle the numbers that are between 494 and 508.

512   492

406

499

504

Circle the amounts that are more than £1.00.

76p   £0.35

£1.28   £1.79

104p

Circle the amounts that are less than £2.50.

309p   £1.76

£3.05

£2.38   245p

Circle the amounts that are between £1.80 and £2.00.

167p   190p

£2.94

183p

£1.79

Adding and subtracting

Write the answer to each sum.

99	248	990	1 856
+ 1	+ 10	− 1	− 10
100	258	989	1 846

Add 1 to each of these numbers.

18		27		78		99	
147		189		203		366	
499		509		1 601		4 750	

Add 10 to each of these numbers.

46		78		43		29	
82		112		156		190	
205		256		397		402	
500		564		672		790	
803		865		894		992	

Subtract 1 from each of these numbers.

17		24		30		56	
79		90		149		200	
50		4 235		3 890		5 236	

Subtract 10 from each of these numbers.

54		83		100		175	
190		206		367		500	
631		701		740		799	
840		900		3 654		2 450	
9 000		6 060		3 507		128	

Adding

Write the answer to each sum.

21 + 14 + 15 = 50   16 + 12 + 20 = 48

Write the answer to each sum.

25 + 30 + 20 =   60 + 25 + 15 =   14 + 16 + 30 =

72 + 12 + 10 =   35 + 15 + 30 =   30 + 13 + 14 =

23 + 24 + 30 =   42 + 16 + 20 =   21 + 40 + 34 =

32 + 10 + 45 =   30 + 34 + 21 =   15 + 15 + 60 =

12 + 13 + 14 =   10 + 11 + 12 =   13 + 14 + 13 =

15 + 25 + 35 =   25 + 35 + 7 =   24 + 14 + 7 =

41 + 22 + 7 =   42 + 13 + 4 =   26 + 14 + 7 =

62 + 8 + 11 =   45 + 21 + 12 =   13 + 15 + 6 =

40 + 30 + 20 =   50 + 40 + 20 =   30 + 40 + 50 =

8 + 18 + 80 =   25 + 45 + 8 =   43 + 34 + 6 =

22 + 33 + 44 =   13 + 70 + 11 =   16 + 14 + 60 =

17 + 13 + 60 =   24 + 26 + 50 =   31 + 19 + 20 =

Write the answer to each sum.

6 + 7 + 8 + 9 =   4 + 6 + 8 + 10 =

3 + 5 + 7 + 9 =   8 + 9 + 10 + 11 =

1 + 4 + 7 + 11 =   8 + 6 + 4 + 2 =

10 + 7 + 5 + 2 =   9 + 7 + 5 + 3 =

Adding

Write the answer in the box.

$$\begin{array}{r} 34 \\ +\ 13 \\ \hline \boxed{47} \end{array}$$
$$\begin{array}{r} 26 \\ +\ 12 \\ \hline \boxed{38} \end{array}$$
$$\begin{array}{r} 41 \\ +\ 14 \\ \hline \boxed{55} \end{array}$$

Work out each addition using the same method.

$$\begin{array}{r} 45 \\ +\ 24 \\ \hline \end{array}$$
$$\begin{array}{r} 31 \\ +\ 18 \\ \hline \end{array}$$
$$\begin{array}{r} 53 \\ +\ 26 \\ \hline \end{array}$$
$$\begin{array}{r} 62 \\ +\ 16 \\ \hline \end{array}$$
$$\begin{array}{r} 37 \\ +\ 10 \\ \hline \end{array}$$

$$\begin{array}{r} 26 \\ +\ 13 \\ \hline \end{array}$$
$$\begin{array}{r} 72 \\ +\ 15 \\ \hline \end{array}$$
$$\begin{array}{r} 39 \\ +\ 10 \\ \hline \end{array}$$
$$\begin{array}{r} 24 \\ +\ 15 \\ \hline \end{array}$$
$$\begin{array}{r} 52 \\ +\ 17 \\ \hline \end{array}$$

$$\begin{array}{r} 36 \\ +\ 13 \\ \hline \end{array}$$
$$\begin{array}{r} 56 \\ +\ 14 \\ \hline \end{array}$$
$$\begin{array}{r} 12 \\ +\ 16 \\ \hline \end{array}$$
$$\begin{array}{r} 67 \\ +\ 11 \\ \hline \end{array}$$
$$\begin{array}{r} 54 \\ +\ 16 \\ \hline \end{array}$$

$$\begin{array}{r} 326 \\ +126 \\ \hline \end{array}$$
$$\begin{array}{r} 456 \\ +327 \\ \hline \end{array}$$
$$\begin{array}{r} 738 \\ +123 \\ \hline \end{array}$$
$$\begin{array}{r} 529 \\ +324 \\ \hline \end{array}$$
$$\begin{array}{r} 337 \\ +227 \\ \hline \end{array}$$

$$\begin{array}{r} 428 \\ +217 \\ \hline \end{array}$$
$$\begin{array}{r} 319 \\ +326 \\ \hline \end{array}$$
$$\begin{array}{r} 626 \\ +138 \\ \hline \end{array}$$
$$\begin{array}{r} 456 \\ +144 \\ \hline \end{array}$$
$$\begin{array}{r} 536 \\ +276 \\ \hline \end{array}$$

Subtracting

Write the answer in the box.

54 − 12 = 42   51 − 21 = 30

Write the answer in the box.

32 − 17 =	48 − 16 =	53 − 21 =	57 − 33 =
70 − 26 =	42 − 24 =	64 − 25 =	73 − 27 =
64 − 38 =	73 − 26 =	43 − 26 =	70 − 34 =
47 − 26 =	62 − 26 =	34 − 18 =	90 − 36 =
63 − 48 =	54 − 37 =	63 − 47 =	73 − 56 =

Write the answer in the box.

72p − 36p =	41p − 23p =	53p − 46p =	60p − 46p =
74p − 39p =	76p − 34p =	84p − 36p =	91p − 41p =
75p − 35p =	66p − 28p =	78p − 43p =	45p − 35p =
83p − 67p =	44p − 39p =	59p − 38p =	44p − 37p =
90p − 26p =	79p − 29p =	54p − 26p =	65p − 37p =

Write the answer in the box.

Reduce 70p by 23p.

Take 46p away from £1.00.

How much is 85p minus 46p?

Take away 47p from 94p.

What is the difference between 56p and £1.00?

How much less than 72 cm is 36 cm?

Miah has 60p and spends 32p on sweets. How much does she have left?

Reduce 94 cm by 48 cm.

Subtracting

Write the answer in the box.

73	45	72
− 48	− 26	− 36
25	19	36

Write the answer in the box.

67	43	63	72
− 48	− 26	− 46	− 45

71	82	63	90
− 47	− 36	− 44	− 47

80	90	65	81
− 46	− 63	− 37	− 47

Write the answer in the box.

46 cm	59 cm	74 cm	60 cm
− 18 cm	− 36 cm	− 27 cm	− 44 cm

70 cm	54 cm	39 cm	91 cm
− 47 cm	− 26 cm	− 4 cm	− 47 cm

Write the answer in the box.

43p	61p	73p	71p
− 17p	− 24p	− 36p	− 46p

470p	381p	563p	474p
−144p	−237p	−246p	−144p

690 cm	494 cm	196 cm	698 cm
−234 cm	−247 cm	− 78 cm	− 345 cm

Multiples

Circle the numbers in the 2 x table.

1　3
6　4
5　2

Circle the numbers in the 2 x table.

17　18　23　21　20
22　19　24

Circle the numbers in the 2 x table.

26　90　87
47　36
44　61　53

Circle the numbers in the 5 x table.

15　40　47
10　3
24　18　50

Circle the numbers in the 5 x table.

76　85　91
47　48
90　65　60

Circle the numbers in the 10 x table.

24　40　44
20　58
15　1　60

Circle the numbers in the 10 x table.

260　605
70　400
110　99

Multiplying

Write the answer in the box.

7 x 3 = `21`   9 x 5 = `45`   6 x 10 = `60`

Write the answer in the box.

2 x 3 = ___   7 x 4 = ___   4 x 3 = ___   6 x 4 = ___

9 x 5 = ___   8 x 3 = ___   6 x 3 = ___   10 x 9 = ___

3 x 2 = ___   9 x 4 = ___   7 x 5 = ___   5 x 4 = ___

0 x 3 = ___   8 x 4 = ___   4 x 10 = ___   0 x 4 = ___

5 x 3 = ___   4 x 4 = ___   9 x 3 = ___   8 x 5 = ___

Write the answer in the box.

Three times a number is 18. ___
What is the number?

A number multiplied by 4 is 36. ___
What is the number?

A child draws 8 squares.
How many sides
have to be drawn? ___

Light bulbs come in packets of 3.
A lady buys 6 packets. How
many bulbs will she have? ___

Mari is given eight 5p coins.
How much money
is she given? ___

A box contains 4 tins of beans.
A man buys 9 boxes. How
many tins does he have? ___

A girl is given 3p for every point
she gains in a spelling test.
How much will she receive if
she gets 10 points? ___

Four times a number is 24. ___
What is the number?

A bottle holds 4 litres of
squash. How much will 7
bottles hold? ___

Six times a number is 30. ___
What is the number?

Dividing

Work out each division problem.
Some will have remainders, some will not.

$15 \div 3 =$ 5

$17 \div 4 =$ 4 r 1

5 r 1
$2\overline{)11}$

2 r 2
$3\overline{)8}$

Work out each division problem. Some will have remainders, some will not.

$26 \div 3 =$ $31 \div 4 =$ $18 \div 10 =$ $24 \div 6 =$

$17 \div 4 =$ $24 \div 5 =$ $37 \div 10 =$ $28 \div 4 =$

$40 \div 10 =$ $26 \div 4 =$ $42 \div 4 =$ $12 \div 5 =$

$7 \div 3 =$ $24 \div 3 =$ $35 \div 10 =$ $56 \div 10 =$

$3 \div 2 =$ $25 \div 4 =$ $29 \div 4 =$ $44 \div 4 =$

Work out each division problem. Some will have remainders, some will not.

$4\overline{)16}$ $5\overline{)32}$ $3\overline{)10}$ $5\overline{)13}$

$4\overline{)14}$ $3\overline{)21}$ $10\overline{)70}$ $3\overline{)19}$

$5\overline{)17}$ $4\overline{)32}$ $2\overline{)22}$ $5\overline{)36}$

Work out the answer to each problem.

23 carrots are shared equally by 4 rabbits.
How many carrots does each rabbit receive
and how many are left over?

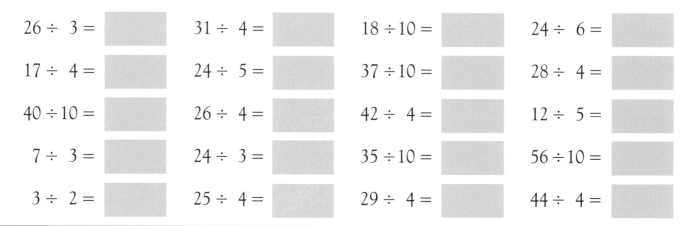

36 apples are shared equally between 5 horses.
How many apples does each horse receive and
how many are left over?

12

Choose the operation

Put either + or – in the box to make each sum correct.

20 $\boxed{+}$ 13 = 33   24 $\boxed{-}$ 18 = 6   17 $\boxed{+}$ 14 = 31

Put either + or – in the box to make each sum correct.

15 ▢ 19 = 34   21 ▢ 9 = 12   16 ▢ 11 = 5   29 ▢ 23 = 52

60 ▢ 25 = 35   45 ▢ 18 = 63   65 ▢ 30 = 35   42 ▢ 18 = 60

71 ▢ 36 = 107   60 ▢ 37 = 23   57 ▢ 12 = 45   66 ▢ 16 = 82

59 ▢ 20 = 39   72 ▢ 40 = 32   84 ▢ 32 = 52   38 ▢ 38 = 76

29 ▢ 29 = 0   45 ▢ 45 = 90   29 ▢ 45 = 74   73 ▢ 16 = 57

Write the answer in the box.

I add 26 to a number and the answer is 50. What number did I start with? ▢

67 added to a number makes 80. What is the number? ▢

36 added to a number gives a total of 64. What is the number? ▢

I subtract 18 from a number and the result is 24. What number did I start with? ▢

I take 22 away from a number and have 15 left. What number did I start with? ▢

Two numbers add up to 50. One of the numbers is 26. What is the other number? ▢

Two numbers are added together and the total is 84. One of the numbers is 66. What is the other number? ▢

After spending 34p, I have 65p left. How much did I start with? ▢

Write + or – in the box.

17p ▢ 35p = 52p   46p ▢ 37p = 9p   72p ▢ 31p = 41p

68p ▢ 68p = 0p   25p ▢ 3p = 22p   80p ▢ 46p = 34p

74p ▢ 20p = 94p   28p ▢ 14p = 42p   52p ▢ 17p = 35p

53p ▢ 24p = 77p   63p ▢ 27p = 36p   56p ▢ 23p = 79p

Choose the operation

Put either x or ÷ in the box to make each sum correct.

$7 \times 4 = 28$ $24 \div 4 = 6$ $60 \div 10 = 6$

Put either x or ÷ in the box.

$6 \;\square\; 4 = 24$ $28 \;\square\; 4 = 7$ $30 \;\square\; 10 = 3$ $9 \;\square\; 3 = 27$

$35 \;\square\; 5 = 7$ $18 \;\square\; 3 = 6$ $24 \;\square\; 3 = 8$ $40 \;\square\; 10 = 4$

$20 \;\square\; 4 = 5$ $30 \;\square\; 5 = 6$ $3 \;\square\; 7 = 21$ $25 \;\square\; 5 = 5$

$3 \;\square\; 5 = 15$ $5 \;\square\; 9 = 45$ $8 \;\square\; 4 = 2$ $12 \;\square\; 3 = 4$

$4 \;\square\; 4 = 16$ $5 \;\square\; 10 = 50$ $45 \;\square\; 9 = 5$ $7 \;\square\; 8 = 56$

Write the answer in the box.

A number divided by 3 is 7.
What is the number?

A number divided by 6 is 3.
What is the number?

A number multiplied by 4
gives the answer 0. What is
the number?

I multiply a number by 5
and the answer is 45.
What is the number?

I multiply a number by 8 and the
result is 32. What is the number?

A number multiplied by 6 is 18.
What is the number?

I divide a number by 3 and the
result is 10. What is the number?

I divide a number by 7 and the
answer is 3. What is the number?

Write x or ÷ in the box.

$50 \;\square\; 10 = 5$ $4 \;\square\; 25 = 100$ $33 \;\square\; 3 = 11$

$3 \;\square\; 3 = 1$ $3 \;\square\; 3 = 9$ $300 \;\square\; 3 = 100$

$44 \;\square\; 4 = 11$ $200 \;\square\; 5 = 40$ $100 \;\square\; 4 = 400$

$45 \;\square\; 9 = 5$ $36 \;\square\; 9 = 4$ $4 \;\square\; 0 = 0$

$200 \;\square\; 10 = 20$ $300 \;\square\; 5 = 60$ $90 \;\square\; 3 = 30$

Working with coins

Write the answers in the boxes.

Sarah has 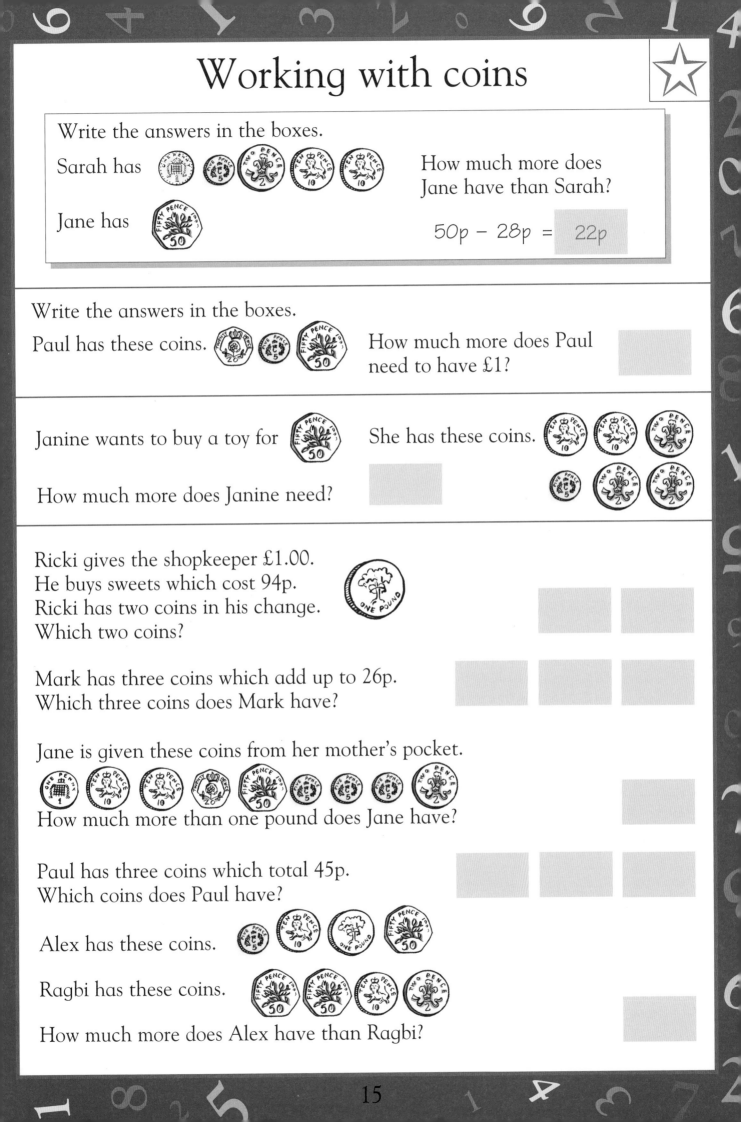 a penny, a five pence, a two pence, a ten pence, a ten pence.

Jane has a fifty pence coin.

How much more does Jane have than Sarah?

50p − 28p = 22p

Write the answers in the boxes.

Paul has these coins. (twenty pence, five pence, fifty pence)

How much more does Paul need to have £1?

Janine wants to buy a toy for (fifty pence). She has these coins. (ten pence, ten pence, two pence, five pence, two pence, two pence)

How much more does Janine need?

Ricki gives the shopkeeper £1.00.
He buys sweets which cost 94p.
Ricki has two coins in his change.
Which two coins?

Mark has three coins which add up to 26p.
Which three coins does Mark have?

Jane is given these coins from her mother's pocket.
(one penny, ten pence, ten pence, twenty pence, fifty pence, five pence, five pence, five pence, two pence)
How much more than one pound does Jane have?

Paul has three coins which total 45p.
Which coins does Paul have?

Alex has these coins. (five pence, ten pence, one pound, fifty pence)

Ragbi has these coins. (fifty pence, fifty pence, ten pence, two pence)

How much more does Alex have than Ragbi?

Money problems

How much needs to be added to 65p to make £1.00?   `35p`

What is the total of    `50p`

Write the answer in the box.

How many 5p coins are needed to make a total of 50p?

One pound is shared equally by four children. How much do they each receive?

How much is three lots of 15p?

How many lots of £2.50 are equal to £10.00?

Andrea spends £1.63 and gives the shopkeeper £2.00. How much change does she receive?

After spending £1.50, Andrew has 90p left. How much did Andrew start with?

How many 20p coins are equal to £1.00?

Julie has £2.60 and is given £2.40. How much does Julie have now?

Wendy needs £5.00 for a T-shirt but only has £1.60. How much more does Wendy need?

Sean has £2.05 but needs £4.00 to buy a toy. How much more does Sean need?

Write the answer in the box.

10p x 6 =	50p x 3 =	15p x 6 =
12p x 5 =	50p x 10 =	80p – 35p =
65p + 45p =	27p x 3 =	56p – 49p =
50p x 6 =	80p – 33p =	60p x 4 =
£1.30 – 50p =	£2.00 – £1.20 =	£2.60 x 2 =

16

Fractions of shapes

Shade half of each shape.

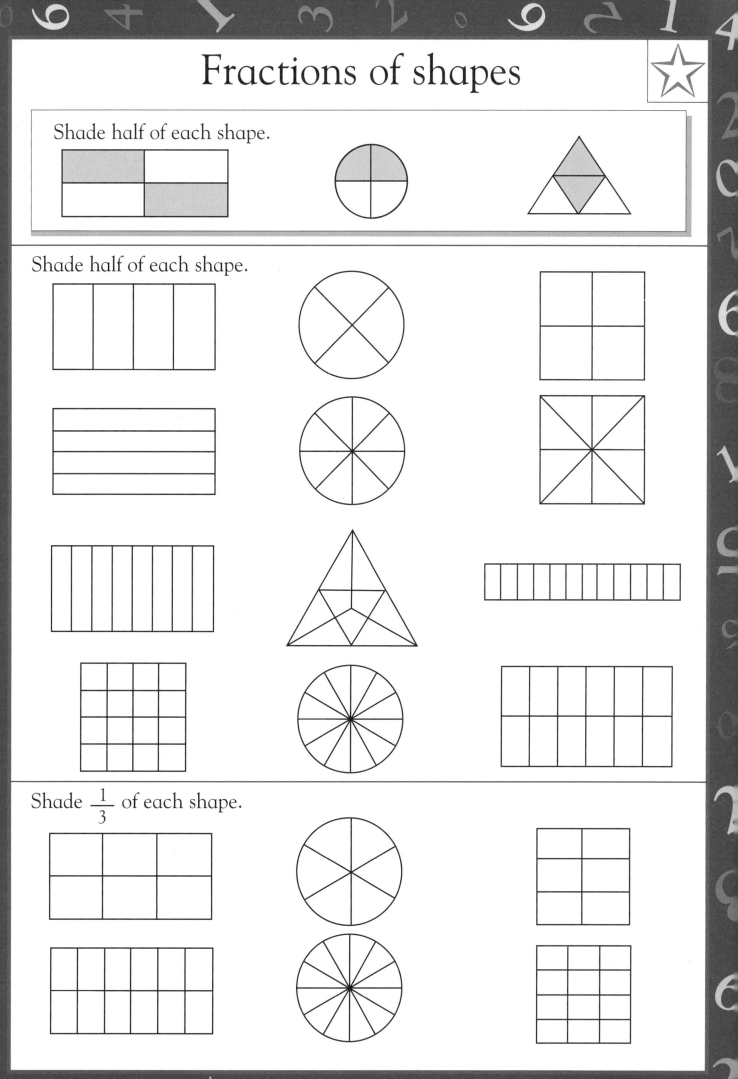

Shade half of each shape.

Shade $\frac{1}{3}$ of each shape.

Fractions

$\frac{1}{2}$ of 12 is **6** $\frac{1}{3}$ of 9 is **3** $\frac{1}{4}$ of 20 is **5**

What is $\frac{1}{2}$ of each number?

4		8		10		2	
6		12		20		16	
14		50		100		60	

What is $\frac{1}{3}$ of each number?

6		12		18		9	
3		15		21		30	
24		60		27		33	

What is $\frac{1}{4}$ of each number?

8		16		4		12	
20		40		80		1	

What is $\frac{1}{8}$ of each number?

16		8		24		40	
32		48		80		56	

What is $\frac{1}{10}$ of each number?

20		40		80		100	
10		30		50		90	

Decimals

Write each amount as pounds and pence.

340p		212p		451p	
175p		63p		1200p	
860p		350p		2000p	
734p		1150p		1450p	

Write each amount as pence.

£2.97		£7.85		£5.05	
£7.09		£6.00		£9.55	
£10.00		£12.50		£9.80	
£15.00		£18.50		£22.50	

Write each length as centimetres.

1.67 m		2.43 m		5.26 m	
2.89 m		7.35 m		8.21 m	
4.27 m		9.52 m		7.04 m	
8.30 m		12.00 m		15.00 m	

Write each length as metres.

244 cm		175 cm		508 cm	
638 cm		410 cm		730 cm	
902 cm		1300 cm		47 cm	
120 cm		24 cm		203 cm	

Telling the time

What time does each clock or watch show?

20 to 6

Quarter past 9

What time does each clock or watch show?

Join the clocks to the watches with the same time.

Telling the time

Show twenty past seven on the watch.   Show half past four on the watch.

7:20

4:30

Show each time on the clock and watch faces.

| Twenty past eight | Quarter to six | Ten past two |

| Quarter past three | Five to nine | Five past eleven |

| Ten to four | Half past four | Twenty to five |

| Five to eight | Twenty past six | Quarter to one |

| Nine forty five | Eight thirty five | Six forty |

Time problems

Read this story carefully. Write the answer in the box.

Lani's uncle came to visit her. His flight took two hours. How many minutes did the flight take?

`120 minutes`

Read each story carefully. Write the answer in the box.

Joe went to the pool at 10 o'clock. He swam for 2 hours, then met his coach for 1 hour. What time did he finish the meeting with his coach?

The film begins at 6 o'clock. It is 2 hours long. When will the film end?

Jenny is queueing for popcorn. Four people are in front of her. Each person has to wait about 5 minutes. About how long will Jenny have to wait?

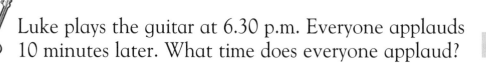

Luke plays the guitar at 6.30 p.m. Everyone applauds 10 minutes later. What time does everyone applaud?

Alan went to the farmers' market at 8.00 a.m. The clock now shows that it's 8.45 a.m. How much time has passed?

Jeremy and Jack go the library at 11.30 a.m. They work on the computers for 20 minutes. They read some books for 20 minutes. They watch a film for 20 minutes, and then they leave. How much time do they spend in the library?

Looking at 2D shapes

Circle the shape that has three sides.

Work out the answers to these questions on shapes.

Circle the shape with four sides that are equal in length.

Circle the shape that has four sides, with two sides shorter than the other two.

Circle the shape that has six sides.

Circle the shape that has more than three sides.

How many sides does a triangle have? Circle the answer.

2   3   6

How many sides does a pentagon have? Circle the answer.

2   5   6

How many sides do each of these shapes have? Write the answer in the box.

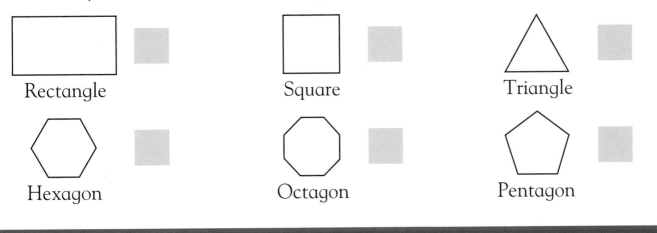

Rectangle   Square   Triangle

Hexagon   Octagon   Pentagon

2D shapes

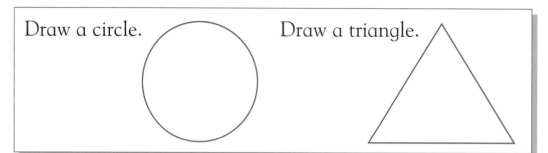

Draw a circle.   Draw a triangle.

Draw each shape as carefully as you can.

Rectangle	Circle	Equilateral triangle

Semi-circle	Regular pentagon	Square

Isosceles triangle	Regular hexagon	Pentagon

Regular octagon	Hexagon	Octagon

Sorting 2D shapes

Are the shapes regular or irregular?

Irregular   Regular   Irregular

Look at the shapes.

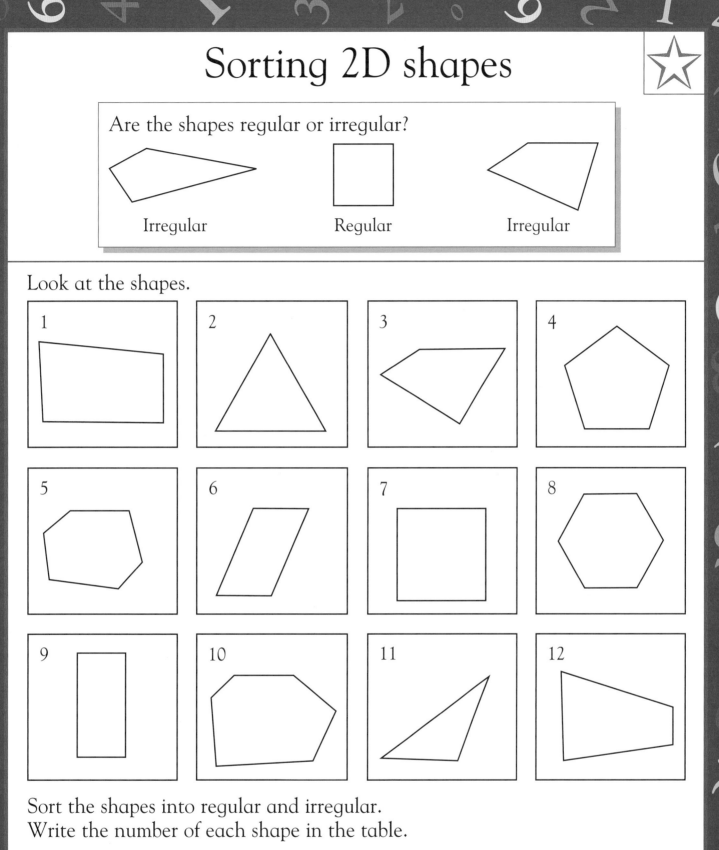

Sort the shapes into regular and irregular.
Write the number of each shape in the table.

Regular shapes	Irregular shapes

Symmetry

Draw the lines of symmetry on each shape.

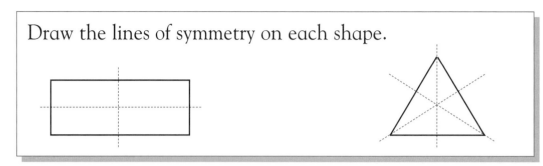

Draw the lines of symmetry on each shape. Some shapes may have no line of symmetry, and some shapes may have more than one line.

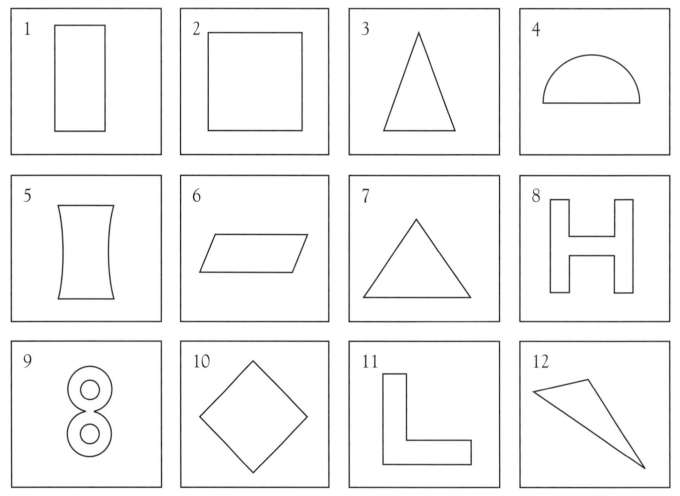

1

2

3

4

5

6

7

8

9

10

11

12

Half of each shape has been drawn as well as the mirror line (dotted line). Draw the other half of each shape.

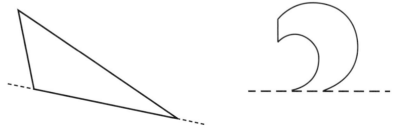

Right angles

Circle the right angles on each shape.

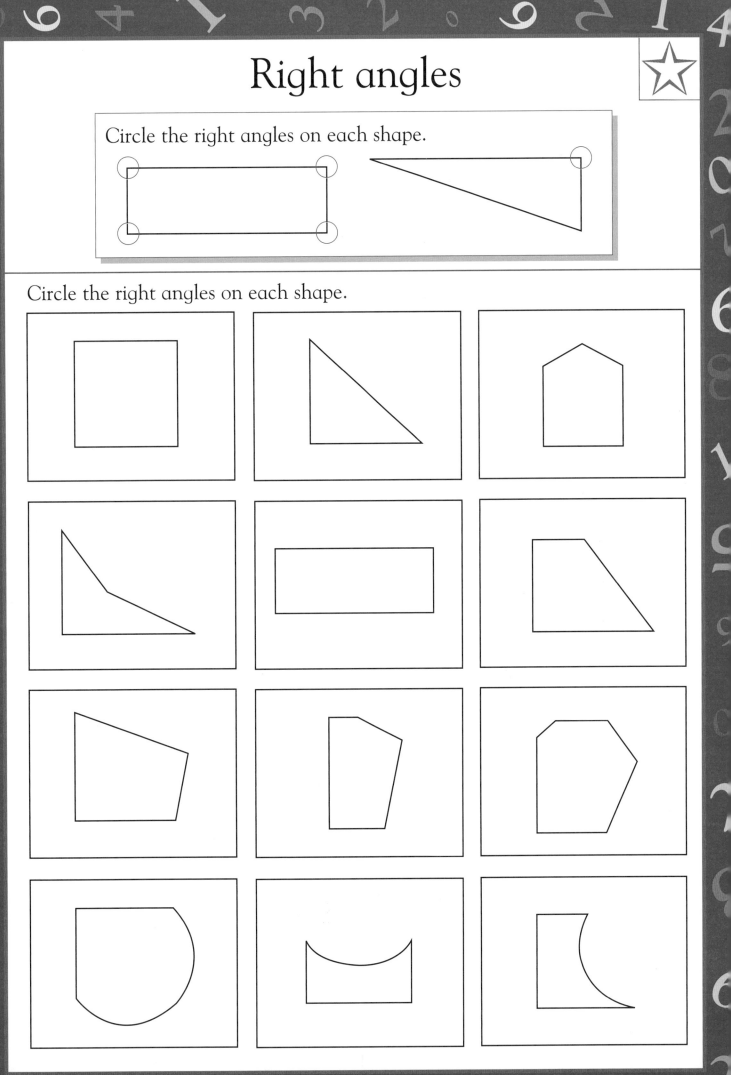

Circle the right angles on each shape.

3D shapes

Write the name of each shape.

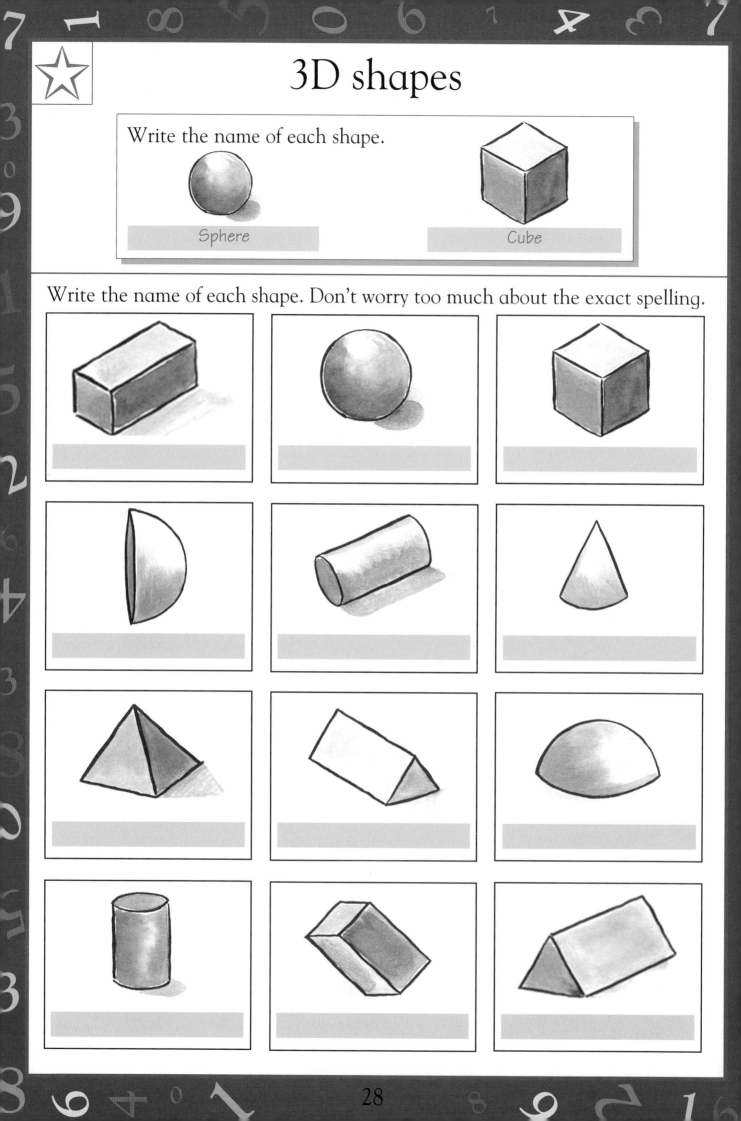

Sphere

Cube

Write the name of each shape. Don't worry too much about the exact spelling.

Sorting 3D shapes

How many edges
does each shape have?

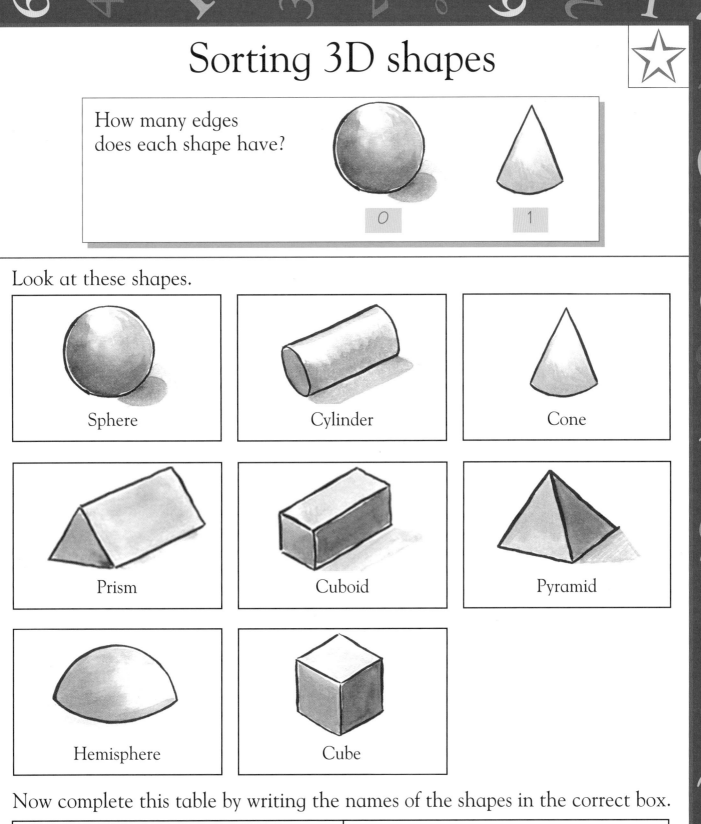

| 0 | 1 |

Look at these shapes.

Sphere

Cylinder

Cone

Prism

Cuboid

Pyramid

Hemisphere

Cube

Now complete this table by writing the names of the shapes in the correct box.

Shapes with less than 6 edges	Shapes with more than 6 edges

3D Shapes

Draw a small circle around each vertex in this shape.

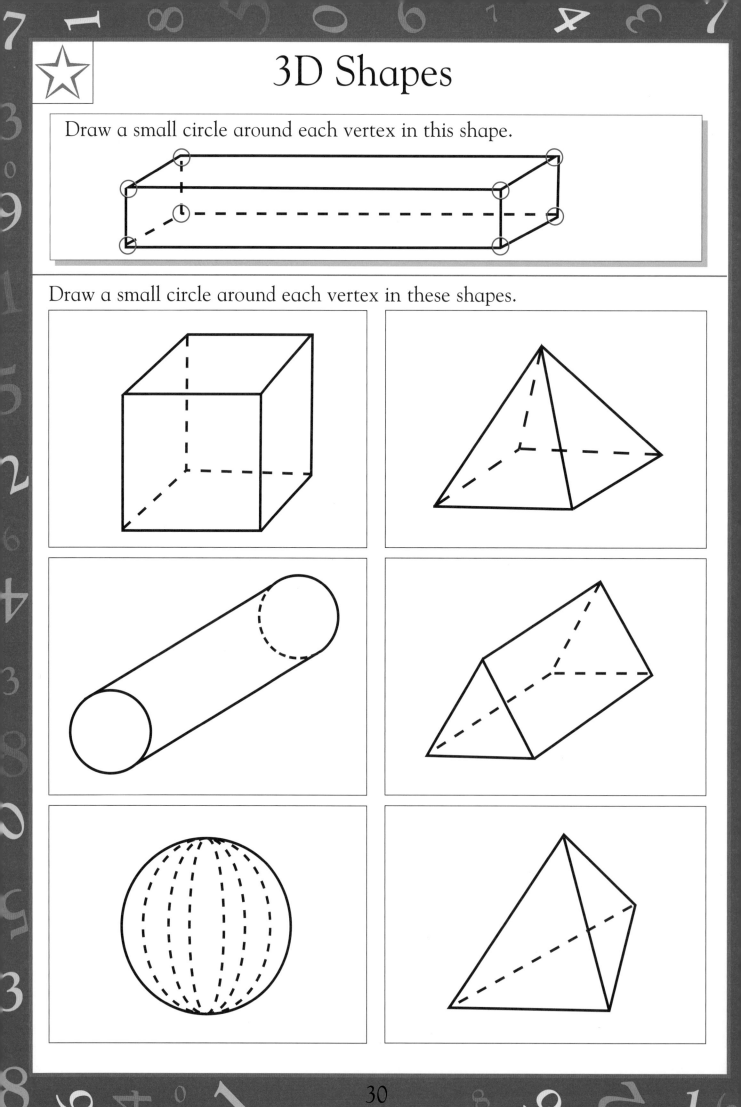

Draw a small circle around each vertex in these shapes.

Pictographs

Look at the information given on the pictograph below.
Answer the questions that follow.

The members of the Smith family are planning to go on a picnic, and discuss their favourite fruits. The children make a pictograph to show how many people like each fruit.

The Smiths' favourite fruit   ☺ = 1 family member

Apples	☺ ☺ ☺ ☺ ☺ ☺ ☺ ☺
Bananas	☺ ☺ ☺ ☺ ☺ ☺
Grapes	☺ ☺ ☺ ☺ ☺
Oranges	☺ ☺ ☺
Strawberries	☺ ☺

How many family members like apples best?

How many kinds of fruit are shown on the graph?

How many people like oranges best?

How many people like strawberries best?

How many more people chose bananas than chose grapes?

Which fruit did six people say they like best?

Bar graphs

The Year 4 students voted for their favourite sports. They drew a bar graph to show the results. Give a title to the graph, then use the graph to answer the questions. Circle your answers.

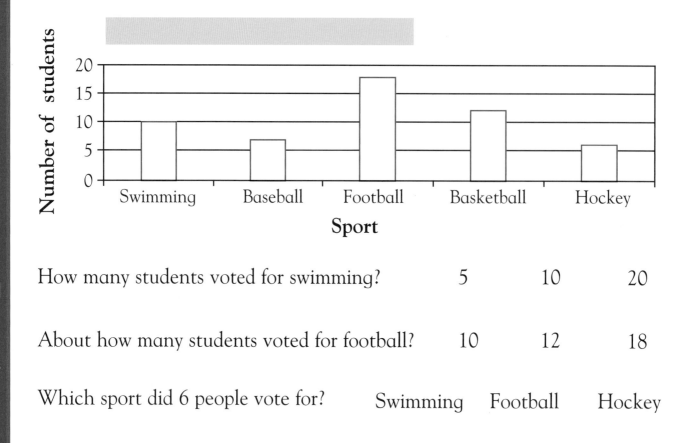

How many students voted for swimming?   5   10   20

About how many students voted for football?   10   12   18

Which sport did 6 people vote for?   Swimming   Football   Hockey

Students at Mayfield School voted for their favourite school lunch:
25 voted for pizza, 18 voted for cheese on toast, 15 voted for chicken nuggets, and 10 voted for veggie burgers. Colour the bars to make a bar graph to show the information.

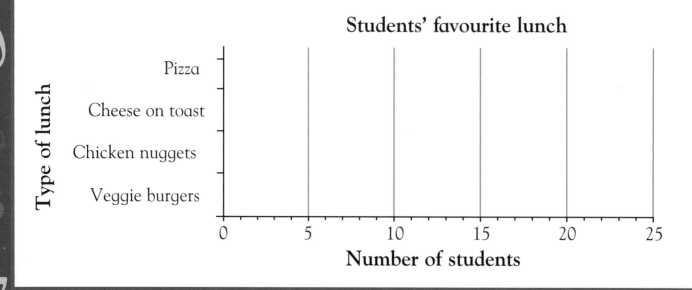

Answer Section with Parents' Notes

Key Stage 2
Ages 7–8
Beginner

This 8-page section provides answers to all the activities in this book. This will enable you to mark your children's work or it can be used by them if they prefer to do their own marking.

The notes for each page help explain the common pitfalls and problems and, where appropriate, give indications as to what practice is needed to ensure your children understand where they have gone wrong.

Counting to 1000

Fill in the missing words and numbers in the boxes below.

250	300	350	400
Two hundred and fifty	Three hundred	Three hundred and fifty	Four hundred
450	500	550	600
Four hundred and fifty	Five hundred	Five hundred and fifty	Six hundred
650	700	750	800
Six hundred and fifty	Seven hundred	Seven hundred and fifty	Eight hundred
850	900	950	1000
Eight hundred and fifty	Nine hundred	Nine hundred and fifty	One thousand

Which number has a value between 456 and 571? Circle the answer.

453   (471)   575   580   600   650

Let children practise writing numbers. Ask them to write numbers as you dictate them, both as words and as digits; for example, one thousand (1000), seven hundred (700), sixty-five (65), and so on.

Comparing and ordering

Write these numbers in order of size, starting with the smallest.

431 678 273 586 | 273 | 431 | 586 | 678 |

Write these numbers in order of size, starting with the smallest.

267	931	374	740	267	374	740	931
734	218	625	389	218	389	625	734
836	590	374	669	374	590	669	836
572	197	469	533	197	469	533	572
948	385	846	289	289	385	846	948
406	560	460	650	406	460	560	650
738	837	378	783	378	738	783	837
582	285	528	852	285	528	582	852
206	620	602	260	206	260	602	620
634	436	364	463	364	436	463	634
47	740	74	704	47	74	704	740
501	150	51	105	51	105	150	501
290	92	209	29	29	92	209	290
803	380	83	38	38	83	380	803
504	450	54	45	45	54	450	504

The exercise tests whether children understand the importance of the position of the digit, that is, whether the digit represents a 'hundreds', 'tens', or 'units' amount. In a mixture of 2- and 3-digit numbers, children might, for instance, confuse 54 and 450.

Comparisons

Circle the numbers that are more than 207.
72   158   (210)   (230)   (208)

Circle the numbers that are more than 705.
(834)   698   (711)   590   (812)

Circle the numbers that are less than 512.
(268)   (507)   600   (378)   564

Circle the numbers that are between 494 and 508.
512   492   406   (499)   (504)

Circle the amounts that are more than £1.00.
76p   £0.35   (£1.28)   (£1.79)   (104p)

Circle the amounts that are less than £2.50.
309p   (£1.76)   £3.05   (£2.38)   (245p)

Circle the amounts that are between £1.80 and £2.00.
167p   (190p)   £2.94   (183p)   £1.79

This exercise tests children's understanding of the importance of position. It also tests their understanding of the format of money when only pence are used. For example, that 104p is the same as £1.04.

Adding and subtracting ⭐

Write the answer to each sum.

99	248	990	1856
+ 1	+ 10	– 1	– 10
100	258	989	1846

Add 1 to each of these numbers.

18	19	27	28	78	79	99	100
147	148	189	190	203	204	366	367
499	500	509	510	1601	1602	4750	4751

Add 10 to each of these numbers.

46	56	78	88	43	53	29	39
82	92	112	122	156	166	190	200
205	215	256	266	397	407	402	412
500	510	564	574	672	682	790	800
803	813	865	875	894	904	992	1002

Subtract 1 from each of these numbers.

17	16	24	23	30	29	56	55
79	78	90	89	149	148	200	199
50	49	4235	4234	3890	3889	5236	5235

Subtract 10 from each of these numbers.

54	44	83	73	100	90	175	165
190	180	206	196	367	357	500	490
631	621	701	691	740	730	799	789
840	830	900	890	3654	3644	2450	2440
9000	8990	6060	6050	3507	3497	128	118

Problems that require carrying over a tens or hundreds column may cause difficulties, for example 499 + 1. Some subtraction sums also require crossing the tens and hundreds barrier.

Adding

Write the answer to each sum.

21 + 14 + 15 = 50   16 + 12 + 20 = 48

Write the answer to each sum.

25 + 30 + 20 =	75	60 + 25 + 15 =	100	14 + 16 + 30 =	60
72 + 12 + 10 =	94	35 + 15 + 30 =	80	30 + 13 + 14 =	57
23 + 24 + 30 =	77	42 + 16 + 20 =	78	21 + 40 + 34 =	95
32 + 10 + 45 =	87	30 + 34 + 21 =	85	15 + 15 + 60 =	90
12 + 13 + 14 =	39	10 + 11 + 12 =	33	13 + 14 + 13 =	40
15 + 25 + 35 =	75	25 + 35 + 7 =	67	24 + 14 + 7 =	45
41 + 22 + 7 =	70	42 + 13 + 4 =	59	26 + 14 + 7 =	47
62 + 8 + 11 =	81	45 + 21 + 12 =	78	13 + 15 + 6 =	34
40 + 30 + 20 =	90	50 + 40 + 20 =	110	30 + 40 + 50 =	120
8 + 18 + 80 =	106	25 + 45 + 8 =	78	43 + 34 + 6 =	83
22 + 33 + 44 =	99	13 + 70 + 11 =	94	16 + 14 + 60 =	90
17 + 13 + 60 =	90	24 + 26 + 50 =	100	31 + 19 + 20 =	70

Write the answer to each sum.

6 + 7 + 8 + 9 =	30	4 + 6 + 8 + 10 =	28
3 + 5 + 7 + 9 =	24	8 + 9 + 10 + 11 =	38
1 + 4 + 7 + 11 =	23	8 + 6 + 4 + 2 =	20
10 + 7 + 5 + 2 =	24	9 + 7 + 5 + 3 =	24

Some strategies to help children work out these sums in their heads are: add the tens and remember them, add the units and then add the two amounts together, look for pairs of numbers which total a multiple of 10. They may use pencil and paper to calculate if necessary.

Adding ⭐

Write the answer in the box.

34	26	41
+ 13	+ 12	+ 14
47	38	55

Work out each addition using the same method.

45	31	53	62	37
+ 24	+ 18	+ 26	+ 16	+ 10
69	49	79	78	47

26	72	39	24	52
+ 13	+ 15	+ 10	+ 15	+ 17
39	87	49	39	69

36	56	12	67	54
+ 13	+ 14	+ 16	+ 11	+ 16
49	70	28	78	70

326	456	738	529	337
+ 126	+ 327	+ 123	+ 324	+ 227
452	783	861	853	564

428	319	626	456	536
+ 217	+ 326	+ 138	+ 144	+ 276
645	645	764	600	812

Most children pick up this method fairly quickly. If good progress is being made, have children try the same method mentally and give them the option of jotting down sub-totals as they go.

Subtracting

Write the answer in the box.

54 – 12 = 42   51 – 21 = 30

Write the answer in the box.

32 – 17 =	15	48 – 16 =	32	53 – 21 =	32	57 – 33 =	24
70 – 26 =	44	42 – 24 =	18	64 – 25 =	39	73 – 27 =	46
64 – 38 =	26	73 – 26 =	47	43 – 26 =	17	70 – 34 =	36
47 – 26 =	21	62 – 26 =	36	34 – 18 =	16	90 – 36 =	54
63 – 48 =	15	54 – 37 =	17	63 – 47 =	16	73 – 56 =	17

Write the answer in the box.

72p – 36p =	36p	41p – 23p =	18p	53p – 46p =	7p	60p – 46p =	14p
74p – 39p =	35p	76p – 34p =	42p	84p – 36p =	48p	91p – 41p =	50p
75p – 35p =	40p	66p – 28p =	38p	78p – 43p =	35p	45p – 35p =	10p
83p – 67p =	16p	44p – 39p =	5p	59p – 38p =	21p	44p – 37p =	7p
90p – 26p =	64p	79p – 29p =	50p	54p – 26p =	28p	65p – 37p =	28p

Write the answer in the box.

Reduce 70p by 23p.   47p

Take 46p away from £1.00.   54p   Miah has 60p and spends 32p on sweets. How much does she have left?   28p

How much is 85p minus 46p?   39p

Take away 47p from 94p.   47p

What is the difference between 56p and £1.00?   44p

How much less than 72 cm is 36 cm?   36 cm   Reduce 94 cm by 48 cm.   46 cm

Children should be able to calculate these subtraction sums in their heads. There are several possible strategies, but one of the most popular is to build up from the lower figure. Encourage children to work out on paper if they need to.

Subtracting ☆

Write the answer in the box.

73 − 48 **25**	45 − 26 **19**	72 − 36 **36**

Write the answer in the box.

67 − 48 **19**	43 − 26 **17**	63 − 46 **17**	72 − 45 **27**
71 − 47 **24**	82 − 36 **46**	63 − 44 **19**	90 − 47 **43**
80 − 46 **34**	90 − 63 **27**	65 − 37 **28**	81 − 47 **34**

Write the answer in the box.

46 cm − 18 cm **28 cm**	59 cm − 36 cm **23 cm**	74 cm − 27 cm **47 cm**	60 cm − 44 cm **16 cm**
70 cm − 47 cm **23 cm**	54 cm − 26 cm **28 cm**	39 cm − 4 cm **35 cm**	91 cm − 47 cm **44 cm**

Write the answer in the box.

43p − 17p **26p**	61p − 24p **37p**	73p − 36p **37p**	71p − 46p **25p**
470p −144p **326p**	381p −237p **144p**	563p −246p **317p**	474p −144p **330p**
690 cm −234 cm **456 cm**	494 cm −247 cm **247 cm**	196 cm − 78 cm **118 cm**	698 cm − 345 cm **353 cm**

These sums require children to 'borrow' from the tens column. The expression 'exchange' is mostly used by teachers when a ten number is removed from the tens and given to the units. The child may use any method that is accurate, but should not use fingers.

☆ Multiples

Circle the numbers in the 2 x table.

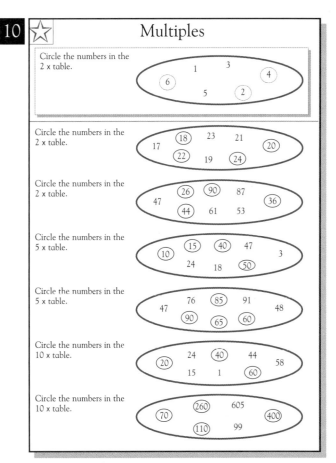

Children should recognise that all even numbers are multiples of 2, however large they are. They should know and understand that all multiples of 5 end in either 5 or 0, and that all multiples of 10 end in 0.

Multiplying ☆

Write the answer in the box.

7 x 3 = **21**   9 x 5 = **45**   6 x 10 = **60**

Write the answer in the box.

2 x 3 = **6**	7 x 4 = **28**	4 x 3 = **12**	6 x 4 = **24**
9 x 5 = **45**	8 x 3 = **24**	6 x 3 = **18**	10 x 9 = **90**
3 x 2 = **6**	9 x 4 = **36**	7 x 5 = **35**	5 x 4 = **20**
0 x 3 = **0**	8 x 4 = **32**	4 x 10 = **40**	0 x 4 = **0**
5 x 3 = **15**	4 x 4 = **16**	9 x 3 = **27**	8 x 5 = **40**

Write the answer in the box.

Three times a number is 18. What is the number? **6**

A number multiplied by 4 is 36. What is the number? **9**

A child draws 8 squares. How many sides have to be drawn? **32**

Light bulbs come in packets of 3. A lady buys 6 packets. How many bulbs will she have? **18**

Mari is given eight 5p coins. How much money is she given? **40p**

A box contains 4 tins of beans. A man buys 9 boxes. How many tins does he have? **36**

A girl is given 3p for every point she gains in a spelling test. How much will she receive if she gets 10 points? **30p**

Four times a number is 24. What is the number? **6**

A bottle holds 4 litres of squash. How much will 7 bottles hold? **28 litres**

Six times a number is 30. What is the number? **5**

The main point about times tables is speed of recall and that children do not use fingers to count. They should be careful when multiplying by 0: the answer is always 0. Children must also realise that if they know 7 x 5, then they also know the answer to 5 x 7.

☆ Dividing

Work out each division problem. Some will have remainders, some will not.

15 ÷ 3 = **5**   5 r 1   2 r 2
17 ÷ 4 = **4 r 1**   2⟌11   3⟌8

Work out each division problem. Some will have remainders, some will not.

26 ÷ 3 = **8 r 2**	31 ÷ 4 = **7 r 3**	18 ÷ 10 = **1 r 8**	24 ÷ 6 = **4**
17 ÷ 4 = **4 r 1**	24 ÷ 5 = **4 r 4**	37 ÷ 10 = **3 r 7**	28 ÷ 4 = **7**
40 ÷ 10 = **4**	26 ÷ 4 = **6 r 2**	42 ÷ 4 = **10 r 2**	12 ÷ 5 = **2 r 2**
7 ÷ 3 = **2 r 1**	24 ÷ 3 = **8**	35 ÷ 10 = **3 r 5**	56 ÷ 10 = **5 r 6**
3 ÷ 2 = **1 r 1**	25 ÷ 4 = **6 r 1**	29 ÷ 4 = **7 r 1**	44 ÷ 4 = **11**

Work out each division problem. Some will have remainders, some will not.

4 4⟌16	**6 r 2** 5⟌32	**3 r 1** 3⟌10	**2 r 3** 5⟌13
3 r 2 4⟌14	**7** 3⟌21	**7** 10⟌70	**6 r 1** 3⟌19
3 r 2 5⟌17	**8** 4⟌32	**11** 2⟌22	**7 r 1** 5⟌36

Work out the answer to each problem.

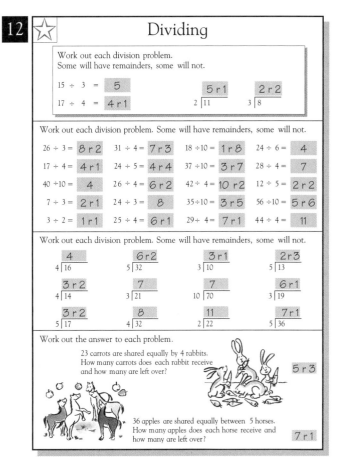

23 carrots are shared equally by 4 rabbits. How many carrots does each rabbit receive and how many are left over? **5 r 3**

36 apples are shared equally between 5 horses. How many apples does each horse receive and how many are left over? **7 r 1**

On this page you may need to explain that not all of the sums can be divided exactly.

Choose the operation

Put either + or − in the box to make each sum correct.

20 + 13 = 33   24 − 18 = 6   17 + 14 = 31

Put either + or − in the box to make each sum correct.

15 + 19 = 34   21 − 9 = 12   16 − 11 = 5   29 + 23 = 52

60 − 25 = 35   45 + 18 = 63   65 − 30 = 35   42 + 18 = 60

71 + 36 = 107   60 − 37 = 23   57 − 12 = 45   66 + 16 = 82

59 − 20 = 39   72 − 40 = 32   84 − 32 = 52   38 + 38 = 76

29 − 29 = 0   45 + 45 = 90   29 + 45 = 74   73 − 16 = 57

Write the answer in the box.

I add 26 to a number and the answer is 50. What number did I start with? | 24

67 added to a number makes 80. What is the number? | 13

36 added to a number gives a total of 64. What is the number? | 28

I subtract 18 from a number and the result is 24. What number did I start with? | 42

I take 22 away from a number and have 15 left. What number did I start with? | 37

Two numbers add up to 50. One of the numbers is 26. What is the other number? | 24

Two numbers are added together and the total is 84. One of the numbers is 66. What is the other number? | 18

After spending 34p, I have 65p left. How much did I start with? | 99p

Write + or − in the box.

17p + 35p = 52p   46p − 37p = 9p   72p − 31p = 41p

68p − 68p = 0p   25p − 3p = 22p   80p − 46p = 34p

74p + 20p = 94p   28p + 14p = 42p   52p − 17p = 35p

53p + 24p = 77p   63p − 27p = 36p   56p + 23p = 79p

The first and third sections are straightforward but the second section requires children to think about whether addition or subtraction is the most suitable way of solving the problem.

Choose the operation

Put either x or ÷ in the box to make each sum correct.

7 x 4 = 28   24 ÷ 4 = 6   60 ÷ 10 = 6

Put either x or ÷ in the box.

6 x 4 = 24   28 ÷ 4 = 7   30 ÷ 10 = 3   9 x 3 = 27

35 ÷ 5 = 7   18 ÷ 3 = 6   24 ÷ 3 = 8   40 ÷ 10 = 4

20 ÷ 4 = 5   30 ÷ 5 = 6   3 x 7 = 21   25 ÷ 5 = 5

3 x 5 = 15   5 x 9 = 45   8 ÷ 4 = 2   12 x 3 = 4

4 x 4 = 16   5 x 10 = 50   45 ÷ 9 = 5   7 x 8 = 56

Write the answer in the box.

A number divided by 3 is 7. What is the number? | 21

A number divided by 6 is 3. What is the number? | 18

A number multiplied by 4 gives the answer 0. What is the number? | 0

I multiply a number by 5 and the answer is 45. What is the number? | 9

I multiply a number by 8 and the result is 32. What is the number? | 4

A number multiplied by 6 is 18. What is the number? | 3

I divide a number by 3 and the result is 10. What is the number? | 30

I divide a number by 7 and the answer is 3. What is the number? | 21

Write x or ÷ in the box.

50 ÷ 10 = 5   4 x 25 = 100   33 ÷ 3 = 11

3 ÷ 3 = 1   3 x 3 = 9   300 ÷ 3 = 100

44 ÷ 4 = 11   200 ÷ 5 = 40   100 x 4 = 400

45 ÷ 9 = 5   36 ÷ 9 = 4   4 x 0 = 0

200 ÷ 10 = 20   300 ÷ 5 = 60   90 ÷ 3 = 30

The second exercise asks children to decide which operation is needed to solve the question, a skill many children do not have as they look at multiplication and division as separate skills, whereas they are opposite sides of the same coin.

Working with coins

Write the answers in the boxes.

Sarah has

Jane has

How much more does Jane have than Sarah?

50p − 28p = 22p

Write the answers in the boxes.

Paul has these coins. How much more does Paul need to have £1? | 25p

Janine wants to buy a toy for   She has these coins.

How much more does Janine need? | 19p

Ricki gives the shopkeeper £1.00. He buys sweets which cost 94p. Ricki has two coins in his change. Which two coins? | 5p | 1p

Mark has three coins which add up to 26p. Which three coins does Mark have? | 20p | 5p | 1p

Jane is given these coins from her mother's pocket.

How much more than one pound does Jane have? | 8p

Paul has three coins which total 45p. Which coins does Paul have? | 20p | 20p | 5p

Alex has these coins.

Ragbi has these coins.

How much more does Alex have than Ragbi? | 53p

Most children should be able to work out correct answers to these sums but the critical point is how quickly the calculations take place. Money is an everyday matter for most people and fast, accurate calculations are essential.

Money problems

Write the answer in the box.

How much needs to be added to 65p to make £1.00? | 35p

What is the total of | 50p

Write the answer in the box.

How many 5p coins are needed to make a total of 50p? | 10

Julie has £2.60 and is given £2.40. How much does Julie have now? | £5.00

One pound is shared equally by four children. How much do they each receive? | 25p

How much is three lots of 15p? | 45p

How many lots of £2.50 are equal to £10.00? | 4

Andrea spends £1.63 and gives the shopkeeper £2.00. How much change does she receive? | 37p

Wendy needs £5.00 for a T-shirt but only has £1.60. How much more does Wendy need? | £3.40

£5.00

After spending £1.50, Andrew has 90p left. How much did Andrew start with? | £2.40

Sean has £2.05 but needs £4.00 to buy a toy. How much more does Sean need? | £1.95

How many 20p coins are equal to £1.00? | 5

Write the answer in the box.

10p x 6 = 60p   50p x 3 = £1.50   15p x 6 = 90p

12p x 5 = 60p   50p x 10 = £5.00   80p − 35p = 45p

65p + 45p = £1.10   27p x 3 = 81p   56p − 49p = 7p

50p x 6 = £3   80p − 33p = 47p   60p x 4 = £2.40

£1.30 − 50p = 80p   £2.00 − £1.20 = 80p   £2.60 x 2 = £5.20

The child should do all the calculations on this page in their head. Familiarity with coins and how to deal with simple problems like these are very important in real life. Children should be encouraged to explain their way of working.

17 — Fractions of shapes

Shade half of each shape.

Shade half of each shape.

Shade $\frac{1}{3}$ of each shape.

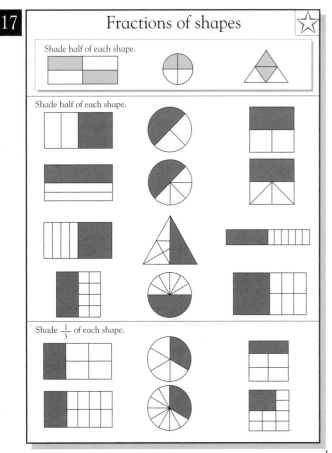

The questions test children's ability to realise that $\frac{1}{2}$ or $\frac{1}{3}$ relates to the total number of sections and that, for example, $\frac{1}{3}$ of 6 is 2. The actual sections shaded do not matter as long as the correct fraction of the total has been shaded.

18 — Fractions

$\frac{1}{2}$ of 12 is	6	$\frac{1}{3}$ of 9 is	3	$\frac{1}{4}$ of 20 is	5

What is $\frac{1}{2}$ of each number?

4	2	8	4	10	5	2	1
6	3	12	6	20	10	16	8
14	7	50	25	100	50	60	30

What is $\frac{1}{3}$ of each number?

6	2	12	4	18	6	9	3
3	1	15	5	21	7	30	10
24	8	60	20	27	9	33	11

What is $\frac{1}{4}$ of each number?

8	2	16	4	4	1	12	3
20	5	40	10	80	20	1	$\frac{1}{4}$

What is $\frac{1}{8}$ of each number?

16	2	8	1	24	3	40	5
32	4	48	6	80	10	56	7

What is $\frac{1}{10}$ of each number?

20	2	40	4	80	8	100	10
10	1	30	3	50	5	90	9

If necessary explain that, to find a fraction such as $\frac{1}{2}$, divide by 2. In the third section the child will need to give a fraction as an answer. The fourth section may be problematic if the child is weak on the 8-times table.

19 — Decimals

Write 210p as pounds and pence. £2.10
Write 1.60 m as centimetres. 160 cm

Write each amount as pounds and pence.

340p	£3.40	212p	£2.12	451p	£4.51
175p	£1.75	63p	£0.63	1200p	£12.00
860p	£8.60	350p	£3.50	2000p	£20.00
734p	£7.34	1150p	£11.50	1450p	£14.50

Write each amount as pence.

£2.97	297p	£7.85	785p	£5.05	505p
£7.09	709p	£6.00	600p	£9.55	955p
£10.00	1000p	£12.50	1250p	£9.80	980p
£15.00	1500p	£18.50	1850p	£22.50	2250p

Write each length as centimetres.

1.67 m	167 cm	2.43 m	243 cm	5.26 m	526 cm
2.89 m	289 cm	7.35 m	735 cm	8.21 m	821 cm
4.27 m	427 cm	9.52 m	952 cm	7.04 m	704 cm
8.30 m	830 cm	12.00 m	1200 cm	15.00 m	1500 cm

Write each length as metres.

244 cm	2.44 m	175 cm	1.75 m	508 cm	5.08 m
638 cm	6.38 m	410 cm	4.10 m	730 cm	7.30 m
902 cm	9.02 m	1300 cm	13.00 m	47 cm	0.47 m
120 cm	1.20 m	24 cm	0.24 m	203 cm	2.03 m

The first two sections may present problems with the number of pence being in thousands. In the second section, there are two sums to look out for because of the position of 0. Be careful that the child does not confuse £5.05 with 550p.

20 — Telling the time

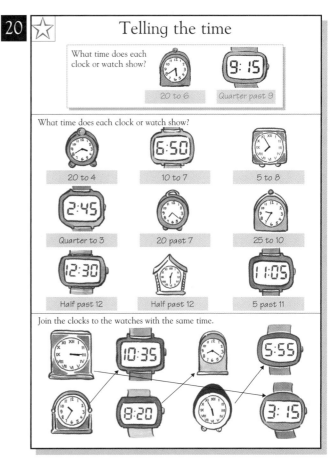

When writing the time children should follow the convention of saying the time 'to' the hour, after half past; so that although 9.35 is not incorrect, 25 to 10 is more usual. Congratulate them if they say a.m. or p.m. on their own.

21 — Telling the time

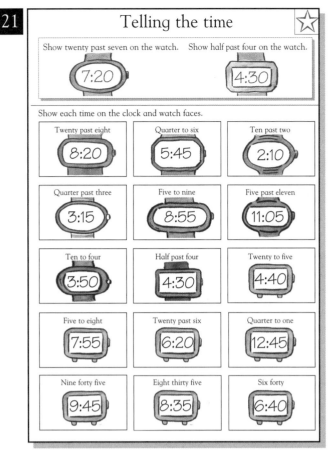

It has been assumed that the times mentioned on this page are in the morning. If children are confident about talking about digital watches that show time on the 24-hour system, then they should be encouraged to do so.

22 — Time problems

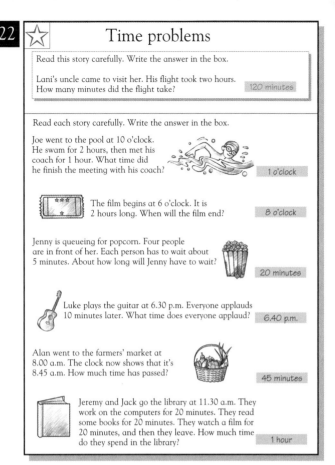

Be sure that children label their answers as minutes, hours, or the correct time as they solve the problems. That will help to ensure that they are making sense of the problems they are solving.

23 — Looking at 2D shapes

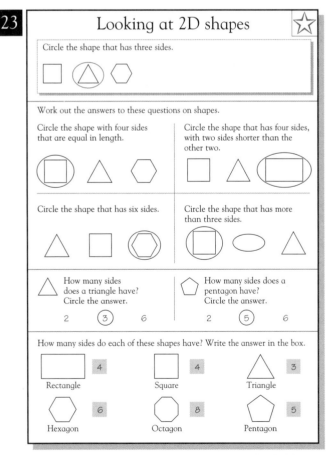

Review the definition of 2-D shapes. Ask children to draw a square on a sheet of paper. Cut out the square. Explain that the square is a flat shape, made up of lines and corners.

24 — 2D shapes

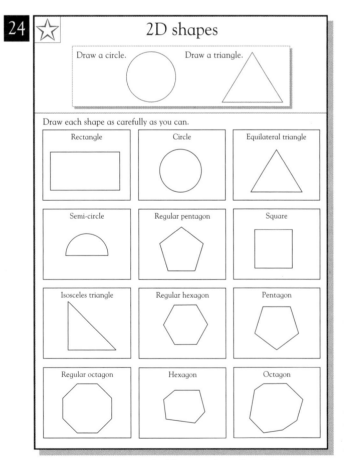

It is important that children realise the difference between shapes that are regular and those that are not. On this page the irregular shapes are simply called by their names (e.g. Pentagon). The word 'irregular' has deliberately not been used.

Sorting 2D shapes

Are the shapes regular or irregular?

Irregular   Regular   Irregular

Look at the shapes.

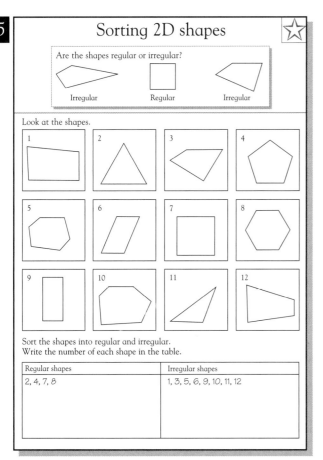

Sort the shapes into regular and irregular.
Write the number of each shape in the table.

Regular shapes	Irregular shapes
2, 4, 7, 8	1, 3, 5, 6, 9, 10, 11, 12

It should be pointed out that regular shapes have all sides of the same length and all internal angles of the same degree. Thus, though a rectangle has all internal angles of 90° it is not a regular quadrilateral since its sides are not equal. A square is a regular quadrilateral.

Symmetry

Draw the lines of symmetry on each shape.

Draw the lines of symmetry on each shape. Some shapes may have no line of symmetry, and some shapes may have more than one line.

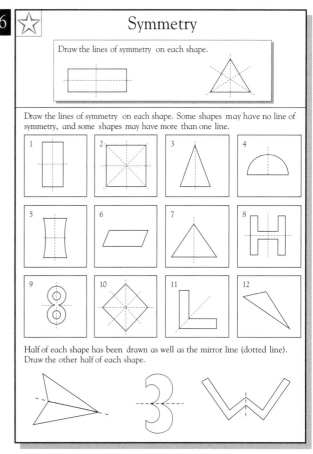

Half of each shape has been drawn as well as the mirror line (dotted line). Draw the other half of each shape.

When children are not very confident they put lines of symmetry on parallelograms. This is not correct and a mirror can be used to show why. Take care with the eleventh shape (with a diagonal line of symmetry).

Right angles

Circle the right angles on each shape.

Circle the right angles on each shape.

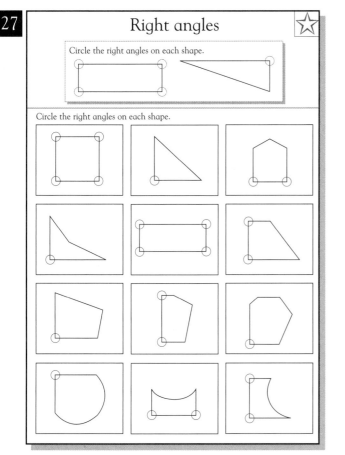

Most of the right angles should be quite clear, but make sure that the children spot all of them, especially on the later images.

3D shapes

Write the name of each shape.

Sphere   Cube

Write the name of each shape. Don't worry too much about the exact spelling.

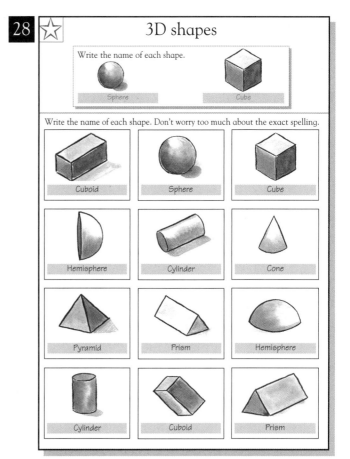

Cuboid   Sphere   Cube
Hemisphere   Cylinder   Cone
Pyramid   Prism   Hemisphere
Cylinder   Cuboid   Prism

Spelling is not important as long as children can say the correct word and know what they mean. Some shapes are given in different orientations because children tend to think of 3D shapes in simple positions. Hemispheres may need to be introduced.

Sorting 3D shapes

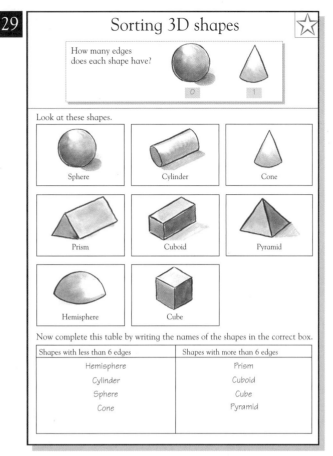

How many edges does each shape have?

0   1

Look at these shapes.

Sphere | Cylinder | Cone

Prism | Cuboid | Pyramid

Hemisphere | Cube

Now complete this table by writing the names of the shapes in the correct box.

Shapes with less than 6 edges	Shapes with more than 6 edges
Hemisphere	Prism
Cylinder	Cuboid
Sphere	Cube
Cone	Pyramid

Children should know that an edge is where two surfaces meet, so a hemisphere has only one edge, where the curved surface meets the flat one. Some shapes are hard to work out from textbooks. Try to make these familiar through real-life objects.

3D Shapes

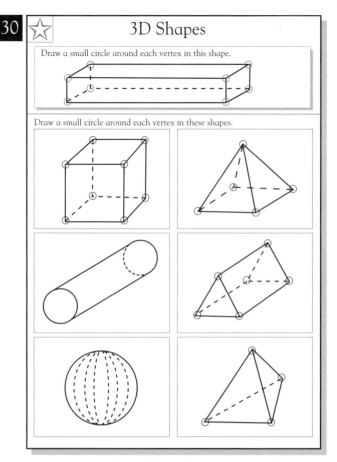

Draw a small circle around each vertex in this shape.

Draw a small circle around each vertex in these shapes.

A vertex is a place where three or more edges meet; you may need to point this out. The cylinder and sphere have no vertices.

Pictographs

Look at the information given on the pictograph below. Answer the questions that follow.

The members of the Smith family are planning to go on a picnic, and discuss their favourite fruits. The children make a pictograph to show how many people like each fruit.

The Smiths' favourite fruit   ☺ = 1 family member

Apples	☺ ☺ ☺ ☺ ☺ ☺ ☺ ☺
Bananas	☺ ☺ ☺ ☺ ☺ ☺
Grapes	☺ ☺ ☺ ☺ ☺
Oranges	☺ ☺ ☺
Strawberries	☺ ☺

How many family members like apples best?   8

How many kinds of fruit are shown on the graph?   5

How many people like oranges best?   3

How many people like strawberries best?   2

How many more people chose bananas than chose grapes?   1

Which fruit did six people say they like best?   Bananas

Creating pictographs can be fun. Encourage children to collect information about friends or family and their favourite colours or foods to create their pictograph. Let them draw pictures to represent food, or faces for people.

Bar graphs

The Year 4 students voted for their favourite sports. They drew a bar graph to show the results. Give a title to the graph, then use the graph to answer the questions. Circle your answers.

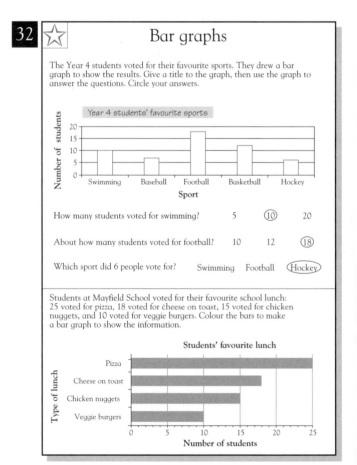

Year 4 students' favourite sports

Number of students
Sport: Swimming, Baseball, Football, Basketball, Hockey

How many students voted for swimming?   5   (10)   20

About how many students voted for football?   10   12   (18)

Which sport did 6 people vote for?   Swimming   Football   (Hockey)

Students at Mayfield School voted for their favourite school lunch: 25 voted for pizza, 18 voted for cheese on toast, 15 voted for chicken nuggets, and 10 voted for veggie burgers. Colour the bars to make a bar graph to show the information.

Students' favourite lunch

Type of lunch: Pizza, Cheese on toast, Chicken nuggets, Veggie burgers
Number of students

Graphs and tables of information help make number concepts more concrete. Graphs also help children understand and compare information. Help your child make a bar graph of your family's favourite games or ice-cream flavours.